W9-ANY-030

DISCARD
WITHDRAWAL

Great Scientific
Questions and the
Scientists Who
Answered Them

HOW DO WE KNOW

THE SIZE OF THE
SOLAR SYSTEM

ISAAC TURIEL

Great Scientific
Questions and the
Scientists Who
Answered Them

HOW DO WE KNOW
THE SIZE OF THE
SOLAR SYSTEM

THE ROSEN PUBLISHING GROUP, INC.
NEW YORK

Published in 2001 by The Rosen Publishing Group, Inc.
29 East 21st Street, New York, NY 10010

Copyright © 2001 by Isaac Turiel

First Edition

All rights reserved. No part of this book may be reproduced in any form without permission in writing from the publisher, except by a reviewer.

Library of Congress Cataloging-in-Publication Data
Turiel, Isaac.
How do we know the size of the solar system / Isaac Turiel.—
1st ed.
p. cm. — (Great scientific questions and the scientists who answered them)
Includes bibliographical references and index.
ISBN 0-8239-3386-5 (lib. bdg.)
1. Solar system—Juvenile literature. [1. Solar system. 2. Astronomers—History.] I. Title. II. Series.
QB501.3 .T87 2001
523.2—dc21

2001000001

Cover images: solar system.
Cover inset: telescope at Yerkes Observatory in Williams Bay, Wisconsin.

Manufactured in the United States of America

Contents

Greek Astronomy

Our ancestors had an interest in astronomy for thousands of years. Even before the Greeks, the Egyptians, Chinese, Indians, and Babylonians made detailed astronomical observations. Some of the constellations we recognize today were named by the Sumerians probably before 2000 BC.

This is an ancient Aztec calendar.

The Babylonians and Egyptians developed calendars and knew that the year consisted of about 365 days. The Egyptians took sightings of the constellations in order to accurately align their pyramids and buildings with the cardinal directions: north, south, east, and west. But these first observations were deeply bound up with religious ideas, and these earliest views of the cosmos were often little more than stories of the gods and how they created the world and intervened in the lives of princes and heroes.

This began to change with the ancient Greeks. The Greeks had their own stable of gods and an

Scientists think the Maya studied the stars at pyramids such as this one, El Castillo at Chichén Itza, Mexico.

elaborate mythology to explain the great mysteries of life. The great Greek poet Homer, who lived around 800 BC, wrote that the earth was like an island floating in a great river. Above, the heavens were an inverted bowl of gleaming "ether." Below the great river was Hades, where the spirits of the dead roamed. But by about the sixth century BC, for educated Greeks at any rate, it was felt that these kinds of beliefs had more charm than truth. Greek sailors used the stars to navigate around the Mediterranean Sea, and they needed more accurate ideas of how the heavens worked. Increasing contact with older civilizations to the east brought to Greece the astronomical knowledge of the Egyptians and others. Schools of "natural philosophy" appeared in which observation and logical reasoning were applied to unexplained phenomena.

The first of these natural philosophers was Thales of Miletus (624–546 BC), generally considered to be the founder of Greek science and mathematics. Little is known about him, but he apparently had access to ancient Babylonian astronomical observations and predicted that a solar eclipse would occur in 585 BC. His contemporaries were astounded when the eclipse actually occurred on May 28 of that year. The Medes and Lydians, about to go to war, were so frightened by the eclipse that they signed a peace treaty and sent their armies home. Other Greek scholars recognized that Thales's prediction meant

Thales of Miletus correctly predicted that a solar eclipse would occur in the year 585 BC.

that physical laws, and not the gods, might govern the heavens. Thales had some strange views. He believed that Earth was a flat disk floating in a vast ocean, and that earthquakes occurred because of the waves and disturbances on the surface of this ocean. Odd though it seems, such ideas are still attempts at rational and empirical explanations, because they do not call upon gods or supernatural forces.

What did these first theorists see when they looked at the cosmos? First of all, in an age before electric lights and illuminated cities, the night sky would have been very dark and the planets and stars more easily visible than today. Both the Sun during the day and the stars at night would be seen to slowly revolve around Earth about every twenty-four hours. Today we are taught from childhood that this is an illusion, and that the stars seem to move because Earth spins on its axis. But the early Greeks, sensing no motion beneath their feet, were justified in assuming that Earth stood still at the center of the cosmos and everything else seemed to revolve around it. A handful of brighter lights in the night sky did not share the motion of the stars, but moved across the sky more quickly, then briefly slid backward in the opposite direction, and then moved forward again.

Pythagoras (560–480 BC), who may have been a student of Thales, taught that Earth was round, but that it stood in the middle of the universe. The brighter lights that moved more rapidly than the stars were other planets, also revolving around Earth. Five planets could be observed with the naked eye by Pythagoras: Mercury, Venus, Mars, Jupiter, and Saturn. But these

Pythagoras believed that Earth was the center of the universe and the other planets revolved around it.

planets, as well as the Sun, the Moon, and the stars, were not thought to be bodies that moved freely. It was believed that they were attached to "spheres," with each celestial body having its own sphere, like a series of concentric glass globes inside each other. This idea was accepted for many centuries. The rotation of the spheres explained why stars and planets moved. Some Greek astronomers at the time of Pythagoras, notably Heraclitus (540–480 BC), thought that Earth rotated on its axis. However, the concepts of Pythagoras prevailed because they were adopted by the great Greek thinker, Aristotle (384–322 BC).

Aristotle, like Pythagoras before him, believed that Earth did not revolve around the Sun. He reasoned that if Earth did revolve around the Sun, that motion should produce an apparent motion of the stars. He believed that we

Heraclitus was one of the few ancient Greek thinkers who believed that Earth rotates on its axis.

would see a shift in the position of the constellations as we swung around the Sun. And then there was the problem of explaining Earth's motion around the Sun, which no one on Earth could feel. All the evidence available to Aristotle favored an Earth-centered universe.

Aristotle did understand that Earth is spherical in shape. He knew that an eclipse of the Moon is caused by the shadow of Earth as it comes between the Moon and Sun. During an eclipse, it was possible to observe the circular shape of the edge of Earth's shadow on the face of the Moon. Aristotle also observed that when we move north or south the positions of the stars in the night sky change with respect to the horizon. In fact, some stars may disappear from view while others come into view. This would be the case if Earth's surface was curved. It was also known that as ships sailed away into the distance, their hulls disappeared before their masts. Conversely, when ships approached, their masts appeared on the horizon before their hulls. The roundness of Earth was not a difficult problem for the Greeks to solve. But the true position of Earth within the solar system was not obvious at first.

Aristotle's influence on later Greek thinkers and on the theologians of the Middle Ages was enormous, and his views of an Earth-centered universe were adopted by the Catholic Church. For many centuries,

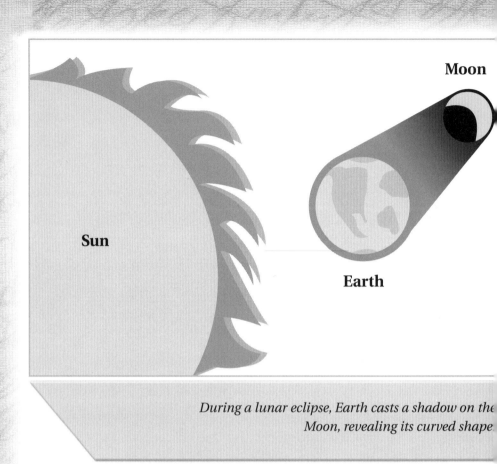

During a lunar eclipse, Earth casts a shadow on the Moon, revealing its curved shape.

the church regarded all other theories as religious heresy. But even in Aristotle's time there were other natural philosophers who disagreed, and who used experiment, measurement, and mathematics to extend our real knowledge of the solar system.

ARISTARCHUS AND ERATOSTHENES

In the third century BC, two Greek astronomers combined observation with geometry to make discoveries about our solar system. Both studied in Alexandria, Egypt, where there was a distinguished scientific school, founded by Alexander the Great in 332 BC. Aristarchus (310–230 BC) was one of the few Greek astronomers who believed that Earth rotated on its axis and also orbited the Sun. He believed that the motions of all the planets could be best explained by this assumption, and because of this Aristarchus is sometimes called the "Copernicus of Antiquity."

Aristarchus was one of the first to try to grasp the size of the solar system, and he devised a clever geometrical method to measure the distance between Earth and the Sun, not the actual distance, but the relative distance. He understood that the

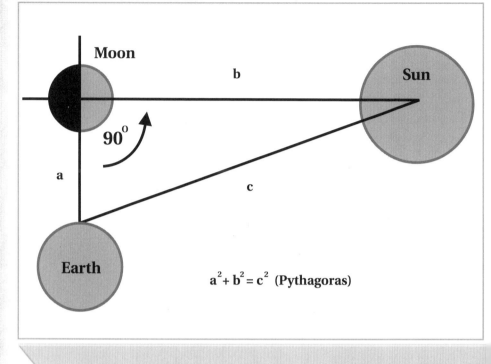

Moon

b

Sun

$90°$

a

c

Earth

$a^2 + b^2 = c^2$ (Pythagoras)

Aristarchus knew that a half-illuminated Moon formed a right triangle with Earth and the Sun.

Moon's brightness was really reflected light from the Sun. He realized that when the Moon was exactly half illuminated, a straight line from Earth to the Moon and one from the Moon to the Sun had to form a right angle. The science of trigonometry was not yet fully developed, and Aristarchus had no instruments that could measure angles very accurately. But the

Pythagorean theorem was well understood, with its postulates about how the angles and sides of a right triangle were related to each other. Aristarchus was able to state that the distance between Earth and the Sun was about twenty times the distance from Earth to the Moon. The true relative distance of Earth from the Sun is about 400 times the distance between Earth and the Moon. Aristarchus's measurements were inaccurate, but his principle was correct, and people began to get the idea that the solar system was much larger in extent than anyone had imagined.

Aristarchus also used an eclipse to estimate that the diameter of the Moon was about one-third the diameter of Earth. The actual diameter of the Moon is slightly more than one-quarter of Earth's diameter, but again, Aristarchus lacked precision instruments to make his measurements. With this information and his calculation of the relative distance to the Sun, he worked out the diameter of the Sun to be about seven times the diameter of Earth. This is of course much too small an estimate. But it was the first time that someone had determined that the Sun was larger than Earth. To Aristarchus, this was additional evidence of a Sun-centered universe, for it made sense to him that smaller objects should orbit larger ones. However, Aristarchus's views were not accepted by most Greeks, and few of his writings have survived. We know of him principally through the writings of others, like Archimedes and Plutarch.

Around 240 BC, the astronomer Eratosthenes (276–194 BC) tried an equally ambitious project, to measure the circumference of Earth. Eratosthenes, a friend of Archimedes, had been put in charge of the famous library of Alexandria by Ptolemy III. He was an all-around scholar, interested in as many different subjects as the great Aristotle. For this reason, he was nicknamed Beta, the second letter of the Greek alphabet, by those who thought he was the second-greatest scholar in the known world.

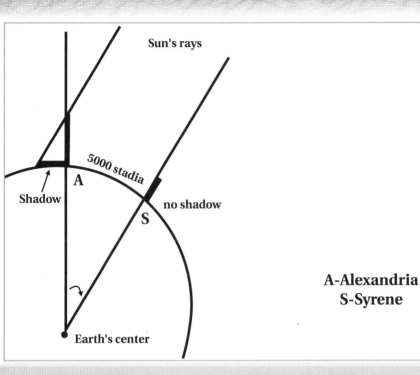

Sun's rays

5000 stadia

A

Shadow

no shadow

S

A-Alexandria
S-Syrene

Earth's center

By measuring the angle of the Sun's shadow from two different latitudes,
Eratosthenes determined what part of the circumference of a
circle separated them.

Eratosthenes knew that at the time of the summer solstice, June 22, the longest day of the year, the Sun was directly overhead and cast no shadows in the southern Egyptian city of Syrene, at the site of Aswan today. At the exact same time, in the more northerly city of Alexandria, the Sun appeared to be seven degrees from the zenith, the point directly overhead, and it did cast shadows. The farther north one went, the lower in the sky the Sun appeared. Eratosthenes reasoned that this was because of the curvature of Earth. The distance between the cities of Syrene and Alexandria represented an angular difference of seven degrees.

If Earth were a perfect sphere of 360 degrees, then the total distance around its circumference was represented by 360 divided by 7, or about fifty times the distance between the two cities. The Greek unit of distance measurement at the time was the stadion (singular) or stadia (plural). Eratosthenes estimated the circumference of Earth to be about 250,000 stadia. Scholars are not certain about the length of a Greek stadion, but the best estimates indicate that Eratosthenes thought Earth was about 25,000 miles in circumference, which is essentially the correct answer.

From this figure, he was also able to calculate Earth's diameter at something less than 8,000 miles.

However, Eratosthenes' calculations were not accepted by other Greek scholars. If he was right, the size of Earth seemed too vast, and too much of it was unexplored compared to the known world at the time. The concept of an Earth that large was just too frightening to contemplate.

HIPPARCHUS AND PTOLEMY

Perhaps the greatest astronomer of ancient Greece was Hipparchus (190–120 BC). Hipparchus established an observatory at Rhodes and created many of the instruments used to study the stars before the invention of the telescope. He plotted the positions of nearly 1,000 stars on one of the first accurate star charts ever created, and he introduced the use of longitude and latitude lines on maps. He also established the first scale for measuring stellar brightness.

Hipparchus also continued the work of Aristarchus in trying to accurately measure the distances from Earth to the Sun and the Moon. He was the first to use the parallax method to determine the distance to the Moon, and to do this he worked out the first accurate table of ratios between the angles and sides of a right triangle.

He is, therefore, often considered the founder of trigonometry. The parallax method relies on measuring the change in viewing angle when an object is observed from two different positions. Depending on how far away an object is, against a background of very distant stars, that object will appear to shift its position when sighted from widely separated observing posts. Knowing both the angular shift and the distance between the observing positions, it is possible with trigonometric tables to determine the distance to the object. That is because when you know the length of one side of a triangle, and you also know the angles that the two other sides make with the known side, you can determine the lengths of the other sides and completely describe the triangle.

That is the beauty of trigonometry. What Hipparchus came up with was a relative value. The distance to the Moon appeared to be about thirty times the diameter of Earth. Though Hipparchus did not make the calculation, Eratosthenes had determined the diameter of Earth to be the equivalent of about 8,000 miles, and thirty times this figure is about 240,000 miles, the correct distance. The Greeks were beginning to develop an accurate understanding of the dimensions of the solar system.

Unfortunately, Hipparchus accepted the dominant view that Earth was at the center of the universe and all other celestial bodies were fixed to spheres rotating around Earth. In fact, he developed a new, coherent, and simplified system for describing the motion of the planets. The problem with the motion of the planets was that they didn't simply revolve around Earth in a straightforward fashion, like the distant stars. Sometimes the planets moved backward in their orbits, a phenomenon called

Over the centuries, the parallax method first used by the Greek astronomers would become the best method for measuring distances to the planets and nearer stars. By measuring the angular shift in position of a celestial body against a background of distant stars when observed from two different positions, it is possible to use trigonometric tables to determine the distance to that body. As objects become more distant from the observer, their angular shift decreases, until they are so distant that no shift is observed. The method then becomes useless, unless the baseline, the distance between the two

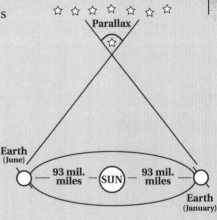

observing points, can be lengthened. What is the longest baseline that astronomers can use? They could build observatories, for example, in London and Beijing, on opposite sides of Earth, with a baseline of almost 8,000 miles. Or they could make one observation in January, and another observation in June, from the same observatory. In the latter case, Earth itself has moved halfway around the Sun in its orbit, creating a baseline between the two observations of more than 180 million miles!

retrograde motion. Today, we understand that this is because Earth, moving more rapidly in a smaller orbit, sometimes overtakes the slower-moving outer planets, so that they appear to move in reverse as we pass them. But if you aren't taught from childhood that Earth revolves around the Sun, this retrograde motion is very difficult to explain. Hipparchus worked out a scheme in which the planets were attached to smaller rotating spheres called epicycles, which were attached to the larger spheres, called deferents. Like wheels spinning within wheels, this system, which seems so unnatural and unwieldy to us today, could be used to predict the orbital position of the planets with some degree of accuracy, if one did not try to project too far into the future. For this reason it was accepted by later Greek scientists, including Claudius Ptolemy (100–170 AD).

Ptolemy's original contribution to astronomy was not great, but because he adopted Hipparchus's Earth-centered solar system, and because few of Hipparchus's writings survive, Hipparchus's ideas are often attributed to Ptolemy, and this view of the solar system is today known as the Ptolemaic system. Ptolemy summarized these ideas in a book that was called *Megale Mathematike Syntaxis*, or "Great Mathematical Composition." Later generations called it simply *Megiste*, or the "Greatest." After the fall of the Roman Empire, Ptolemy's book was preserved in the Arab world, where it came to be called *Almagest*. It was translated back into Latin in 1175 and reappeared in Europe, where the idea of an Earth-centered solar system dominated European thought for another 500 years. One contribution that Ptolemy did make was to ignore the work of Eratosthenes and accept a much smaller and inaccurate estimate for the circumference of Earth. More than 1,000 years later, the Italian mapmaker Paolo Toscanelli (1397–1482), following Ptolemy's estimates, drew a map that put Asia only 3,000 miles to the west of Europe, and he gave that map to Christopher Columbus (1451–1506).

This connection between astronomy and exploration was a very important one. As the ancient civilizations faded away, and as Europe passed through the Dark Ages and into the Renaissance, it was the wealth that could be made from world trade that stimulated voyages of exploration, and explorers needed accurate astronomical knowledge if they were to navigate in unknown waters. Enormous profits could be made simply from knowing the accurate position of a small island in the Java Sea, where pepper or nutmeg might be grown. The needs of trade would sweep away many erroneous ideas, disprove some religious dogma, and open the minds of Europeans to a more accurate view of the universe.

The Heliocentric Solar System

One of the men who would, cautiously, help to sweep away those erroneous ideas was Nicolaus Copernicus (1473–1543). He was born in a little town on the border of Prussia and Poland. When his father died in 1483, he came under the care of his uncle, who was a bishop. His uncle sent him

to the University of Cracow, where he was expected to follow a religious career. However, he became interested in mathematics and astronomy. In 1496 he went to Italy, where he spent the next ten years. In Italy there was a great deal of intellectual activity and questioning of established values, and one important question was calendar reform. Ptolemy's tables were no longer accurately predicting the time of year.

Around 1507, Copernicus began to realize that the mathematical tables then in use, based on the Ptolemaic system, were not very accurate in predicting the positions of the planets over long periods of time. It occurred to him that these tables could be calculated more easily and accurately if they were based on the assumption that the planets, including Earth, revolved around the Sun.

Nicolaus Copernicus believed that Earth revolved around the Sun, but was reluctant to publish his view for fear of persecution by the Catholic Church.

Copernicus's system was far from perfect. It still included a number of the complex epicycles Hipparchus had devised. And Copernicus still insisted that the orbits of the planets were perfectly circular. But he offered a simple explanation for the retrograde motion of the outer planets and other oddities, like the precession of the equinoxes, caused by the slow wobbling of Earth's axis. By 1530, Copernicus had prepared a manuscript containing his radical views, but he was reluctant to publish it. He finally did so in 1543, the year of this death. It was called *De Revolutionibus Orbium Celestium*, or "On the Revolution of the Celestial Spheres." The Catholic Church was sensitive about such radical ideas. A friend added a preface to his book stating that while this might be a useful tool for calculating the future position of the planets, the Copernican theory was not meant to be a real description of how the solar system worked. However, scholars across Europe were not fooled by this denial. The church did not remove Copernicus's book from their list of banned books until 1835.

Tycho Brahe provided the observational data that Johannes Kepler used to measure planetary orbits.

Johannes Kepler (1571–1630) was one scholar who became interested in Copernican theory. Kepler taught at the University of Graz in Austria, but religious tensions in Austria were high during the Thirty Years War, and Kepler, a Protestant, decided in 1598 to move himself to the University of Prague, where he worked under the great astronomer Tycho Brahe (1546–1601). Tycho was one of the greatest observational astronomers to work without benefit of a telescope. He made corrections to almost all existing astronomical measurements. He had estimated the distance to Saturn, the farthest known planet of his time, at 45 million miles, and the size of the whole universe to be about 6 billion miles. While these numbers were not very accurate, they did expand current notions of how big the solar system and the universe were. Brahe used the parallax method to measure distances, using measurements from observatories as far apart as Prague and London, and he used the absence of a measurable parallax to prove that the stars were very far away.

One of the projects that Tycho Brahe undertook was to revise the tables of planetary motion that were working so poorly. When Brahe died in 1630, Kepler inherited all his measurements and data. After careful study of Brahe's observations, Kepler was driven to some startling conclusions. First of all, Copernicus had been right—the simplest explanation that fit the data most perfectly was that the planets revolved around the Sun. The orbits of the planets were not perfect circles, but ellipses, or flattened circles. Furthermore, the speed of a planet in

Kepler's laws of planetary motion supported the theory that the Sun is at the center of the solar system.

its orbit was related to where along the ellipse it was. All this contradicted the fundamental ideas of Greek astronomy and made it impossible to view the planets as being carried along in their orbits by being fixed to circular spheres. But if the planets were not attached to spheres, how did they move? It seemed clear that somehow the Sun was controlling these movements, and for a while Kepler toyed with the idea that the Sun exerted some kind of force similar to magnetism on the planets, but this idea was not pursued.

Galileo demonstrates his telescope to a young Florentine nobleman.

In Prague, Kepler corresponded with another Copernican in Italy, Galileo Galilei (1564–1642). Galileo sent Kepler one of the new telescopes he had built from a Dutch design. It could magnify the heavens more than thirty times, so the era of naked-eye astronomy was over. Galileo was responsible for many discoveries, but his greatest service to the understanding of the solar system

Galileo described the motion of planets around the Sun.

was the principle of relative motion, which explains how the Copernican system could work. The positions of the planets indicated that it was likely that they all revolved around the Sun, and that the apparent motion of the stars was caused by Earth spinning on its axis. But how could that be if no one could feel Earth move, if no one in fact was violently thrown off Earth into space by its rapid motion? Galileo put forward the revolutionary idea that motion could only be felt or measured by someone in a different "frame of reference" from the moving object. If you were part of the same frame of reference, if you were moving along with an object, sharing its motion, and that motion

It should amaze modern readers to see the accuracy of the celestial observations made by the Greeks, or the Egyptians and Babylonians before them, all before the age of the telescope. But the telescope revealed details of the cosmos that revolutionized scientific thinking. The first telescope was built in 1908 by Dutch lens grinder Hans Lippershey in 1608. Lippershey sold some of his telescopes to the Dutch government, which tried to keep the invention secret because of its value in military operations. Galileo heard about the

Dutch spectacle maker
Hans Lippershey designed
the first telescope in 1608.

instrument and built his own. Galileo's was a refracting tele-scope. Light was refracted, or bent, by a glass lens and focused onto a smaller lens, near the eye, that magnified the image. Isaac Newton would

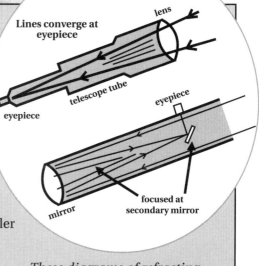

These diagrams of refracting and reflecting telescopes show how each works.

later invent a reflecting telescope, in which the light was focused using a mirror instead of a lens. Reflecting tele-scopes are cheaper and easier to build than refracting tele-scopes, and they have less color distortion.

Telescopes come in all sizes and shapes, but there are some facts that hold true for all types. The diameter of the main light-focusing lens, or mirror, called the primary or objective lens or the primary mirror, is known as the aperture of the telescope. The larger the aperture, the more light the telescope can gather, and the more sharply it can resolve, or distinguish between, objects that are close together. The aperture also determines the useful magnification. A telescope can magnify objects about fifty to sixty times for each inch of aperture. A three-inch refractor, for example, has a useful magnification of 150 times. If an attempt is made to magnify the image more than this, the resolution suffers. The image becomes fuzzy.

The focal length of a telescope is the distance between the primary lens or mirror and the magnifying eyepiece. The exact magnification is given by the focal length of the telescope, usually in millimeters, divided by the focal length of the eyepiece, so that eyepieces with higher magnifications have shorter focal lengths. The focal length of the telescope divided by the aperture gives the telescope's f-ratio. Telescopes with long focal lengths and high f-ratios are capable of higher magnifications, but telescopes with shorter f-ratios provide wider fields of view.

was constant and uniform, you could not detect it. With this principle, he could explain why people and other objects did not fall off a moving Earth, and an important objection to the Copernican theory was eliminated. In 1632, Galileo acknowledged his support for the Copernican system in his book *Dialogue on the Two Chief World Systems*. A year later, the Catholic Church prosecuted him for heresy, and he had to publicly deny what he believed to be true. But among scholars throughout Europe, faith in Greek ideas about the universe finally collapsed. The Sun lay at the center of the solar system, and Earth and the other planets moved around it. There were no heavenly spheres. The planets were solid bodies, like Earth, and some undiscovered force pushed or pulled them through the sky.

THE UNIVERSAL LAW OF GRAVITATION

An explanation for the force that made the planets move was provided by English scientist Isaac Newton (1642–1727) in *Philosophiae Naturalis Mathematica*, or

"Mathematical Principles of Natural Philosophy," published in 1687. It was the product of many years of thought. Newton first became interested in the problem in 1665, as he observed an apple fall from a tree on his mother's country farm. He wondered if

Newton discovered that a force pulled all material objects toward each other, and he calculated how it worked

the force that made the apple fall was the same as the force that made the Moon revolve around Earth. For years he struggled to find a formula that would relate both motions, but his value for the size of Earth was not accurate enough and after a few years he gave up on the problem. Not until 1684, when architect Christopher Wren offered a prize to anyone who discovered this force, did the astronomer and friend of Newton, Edmund Halley, convince Newton to try again. This time he succeeded. There was a force called gravity that acted universally on all objects that possessed mass, that is, every material particle. Gravity was a force of attraction and grew stronger the more massive the objects attracting each other were. It also grew weaker the more distant the objects were in relation to each other. The same equation could be used to explain how rapidly an apple fell to Earth, or how the Moon's orbit curved as it "fell" around Earth, or how Earth revolved around the Sun.

Force itself was a peculiar concept, which Newton defined as an "action at a distance." That is, the effect was felt across empty space between objects that had no material connection. As revolutionary as this idea was, people did have the example of magnetism before them, and so it was not impossible to accept this notion of a pushing or pulling force acting invisibly through empty space. Newton's other laws of motion demonstrated that once this force exerted itself and set an object in motion, as long as no new force opposed that motion, the object would continue in that moving state forever. The heavens worked like a kind of giant mechanical clock, but it was not a clock that needed to be wound in order to keep it going.

Newton recognized that most objects on the surface of Earth lose their energy of motion and come to a stop because their motion was opposed by another force, that of friction. He recognized that in the vacuum of space there was no frictional force, and that the planets would go on revolving forever. No revolving spheres were necessary to explain the motion of heavenly bodies; no mystical explanations were required to explain this unending dance of the planets.

One additional benefit of the law of universal gravitation was that the size or mass of the planets and their distances from the Sun could now be calculated, with the help of Kepler's discoveries about the nature of planetary orbits. If you know the magnitude of the force acting on two bodies and you know how those bodies behave as they rotate around each other, you can calculate their mass and distance. The laws of orbital mechanics enabled scientists to measure the "weight" of the planets through their orbital motions. Thus, the size of the known solar system could be worked out with increasing accuracy.

THE ORIGIN OF THE SOLAR SYSTEM

As the idea of a real, clockwork-like solar system, governed by measurable forces, began to enter scientists' imaginations, many astronomers began to fill in the details with new and improved telescopes. Dutch astronomer Christiaan Huygens (1629–1695) discovered the first satellite of Saturn, which he named Titan, and then, in 1656, discovered Saturn's

Using an improved telescope, Christiaan Huygens was the first to see Saturn's rings

rings. Huygens also made an estimate of the distance to the star Sirius. Incorrectly assuming that it was as bright as and no brighter than the Sun, he put its distance at 2.5 trillion miles. This was only one-twentieth of the correct figure, but it vastly expanded people's conception of the size of the universe. After he settled in Paris in 1669, Italian astronomer Giovanni Cassini

Giovanni Cassini was the first to accurately calculate the distance from Earth to Mars.

(1625–1712) discovered four more moons of Saturn using a telescope that was 100 feet long. He also improved upon Huygen's description of Saturn's ring, showing that it was actually a double ring with a dark gap in between. Using the parallax method and improved telescopes, Cassini first calculated the distance to Mars and then calculated the distance between Earth and the Sun at 87 million miles, only six million miles off the correct distance.

There was, however, a feeling among scientists that, after Newton, all but the details were already known about the solar system. That view was shattered by German-English astronomer William Herschel (1738–1822). With the help of his sister Caroline, Herschel was grinding the finest lenses and producing the best telescopes available in Europe at the time. In 1781, Herschel discovered a new planet, eventually named Uranus, in an orbit even more distant than Jupiter. The discovery sent a shock wave through the scientific community. Herschel had not only doubled the size of the solar system with a single observation, but he had destroyed the apathy felt by many people after Newton's discoveries. There was more, a lot more, to discover. Herschel went on to discover double, or binary, stars. His observations led him to conclude that the dim streak of light known as

William Herschel and his sister Caroline discovered the planet Uranus and doubled the known size of the solar system.

the Milky Way was really a huge disk of stars, of which the Sun and the solar system were a part. He theorized that many of the very distant fuzzy patches of light seen by other astronomers were other collections of stars, galaxies, and galactic clusters at vast distances from Earth. Herschel's view of the cosmos was one in which, for the first time, Earth and the entire solar system became a tiny and not very significant element in a universe too vast to imagine.

How did the solar system come to be? The answer was first suggested by two men, German philosopher Immanuel Kant (1724–1804) and French astronomer and mathematician Pierre-Simon, the Marquis de Laplace (1749–1827). Although he made the suggestion in the endnote of a book on astronomy for a popular audience, as an idea that he himself did not take too seriously, Laplace is generally given credit for the idea over Kant.

Laplace noted that all the planets revolved around the Sun in the same direction, and for

The Marquis de Laplace devised the nebular hypothesis to explain the origin of the solar system.

the most part all had orbits in the same plane in relation to the Sun's equator. He therefore suggested that the Sun and all the planets were formed from the collapse of a huge cloud of spinning dust and gas. Since angular momentum must be conserved, as the cloud collapsed, the inner portion of the cloud would begin to rotate faster than the outer ring, which would be left behind to form a planet. Further contractions would produce more rings, each condensing to form a planet as the inner material continued to condense, until all the planets had been formed, and the Sun formed from the final collapse of the gas cloud. Where Newton had explained the workings of the solar system, Laplace's evolutionary approach provided an explanation for its origin. Laplace called his theory the nebular hypothesis.

The idea became very popular among scientists and assured Laplace's reputation even through the political turmoil of revolutionary France. French emperor Napoleon Bonaparte first made Laplace minister of interior, and then a senator. But after Napoleon's fall, the restored King Louis XVIII did not persecute Laplace, but made him a marquis. We now know, from radioactive dating of the earliest rocks found on Earth, that this condensation from a gaseous cloud occurred approximately five billion years ago.

Another group of theories about the formation of the solar system is now discredited. These are known as catastrophe theories. In these theories, the material that formed the planets was pulled out of the Sun by some catastrophic event, like the close passage of another star or the impact of a comet or a star colliding with the Sun. This idea was first suggested in 1745 by French naturalist Georges-Louis Leclerc, the Comte de Buffon (1707–1788). Since the stars are very far apart, however, such collisions or near passages would be very rare, and very few solar systems would form this way. As we shall see, modern astronomers have reason to believe that planetary systems around stars are quite common.

The Size of the Solar System

ew and improved telescopes making possible more accurate parallax measurements, the development of astrophotography, and a refined theoretical understanding of the nature of the gravitational force all helped to usher in a new age of astronomical discovery in the nineteenth century.

THE SIZE OF THE SOLAR SYSTEM

In 1821, one of Laplace's assistants at the Paris Observatory, Alexis Bouvard (1767–1843), tried to calculate the orbit of Herschel's new planet, Uranus. He found that the actual orbit differed from that predicted by gravitational equations. The problem was not resolved for twenty years, until French astronomer Urbain Le Verrier (1811–1877) and English astronomer John Couch Adams (1819–1892) simultaneously concluded in 1845 that the orbit of Uranus was being distorted by the gravitational influence of another, as yet undiscovered planet. The two scientists were able to predict where in the sky astronomers should look for this new object. On September 23, 1846, at the Berlin Observatory, the planet Neptune was first seen. It was a triumph for the predictive power of Newton's theory.

The last known planet in our solar system, Pluto, was not discovered until 1930 by American astronomer Clyde Tombaugh (1906–1997). In 1929, Tombaugh got a job at the Lowell Observatory in Flagstaff, Arizona. That observatory had been built in 1894 by wealthy

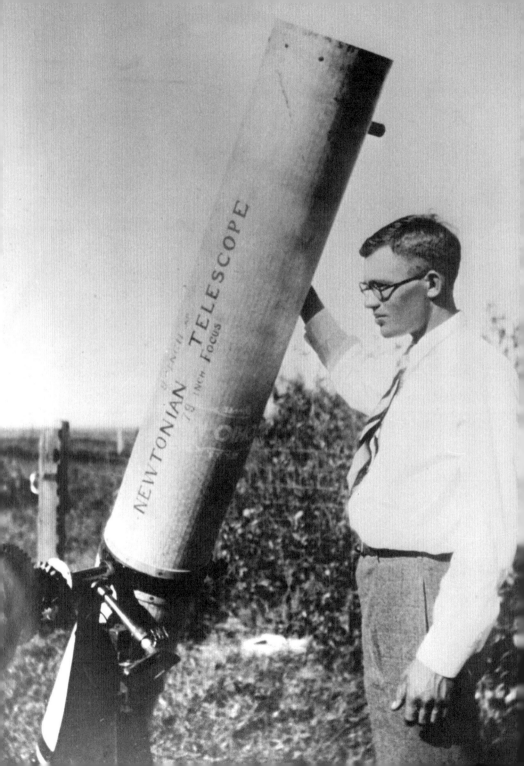

astronomer Percival Lowell (1855–1916) to further his search for intelligent life on Mars. That search proved to be futile, but Lowell also discovered irregularities in the orbit of the newly discovered Neptune and believed that there was yet another distant planet to be discovered. Lowell called it Planet X, and he searched in vain for it for years. Tombaugh took up that search, and the technique he used demonstrates how sophisticated astronomical observations were becoming. Tombaugh would take two photographs of the same section of sky. There were tens of thousands of stars in these photographs. The two pictures were then alternately flashed on the same spot on a screen. Wherever there were only stars with fixed positions, there appeared to be no movement when the two pictures flashed. But a planet, no matter how faint its

Clyde Tombaugh stands beside an amateur Newtonian telescope. He used a more powerful instrument to discover Pluto.

OWELL OBSERVATORY'S

PLUTO DOME
AND
TELESCOPE

ARE BEING PRESERVED
THANKS IN PART TO A
MATCHING
ARIZONA HE...
ADMINISTERED ...
RIZONA STATE HISTORIC
RVATION OFFICE / ARIZONA
STATE PARKS BOARD

PLEASE RETURN
ON WALKWAY

The Lowell Observatory is near Flagstaff, Arizona. Several observatories are based in the American West, where the skies are often clear and there is less light pollution than near large cities.

Percival Lowell

image, would have a different motion from the stars. If there was a planet in the pictures, that object would appear to shift position as the two pictures alternated on the screen. The technique worked, and on March 13, 1930, the discovery of the new planet was announced.

Earth is approximately 93 million miles from the Sun. Before Herschel's discovery of Uranus, Saturn marked the edge of our solar system at a distance from the Sun of more than 890 million miles. The discovery of Pluto moved the outer boundary of our solar system to more than 3.6 billion miles from the Sun.

INFORMATION ABOUT THE NINE PLANETS

Planet	Distance (millions of miles)	Period of Revolution (years)	Equatorial Diameter (miles)	Moons	Rotation period
Mercury	36	0.24	3,032	0	59 days
Venus	67	0.62	7,521	0	243 days
Earth	93	1.0	7,926	1	24 hours
Mars	142	1.88	4,222	2	24 hours
Jupiter	484	11.9	88,846	17	10 hours
Saturn	891	29.5	74,900	22	11 hours
Uranus	1,780	84	31,760	21	17 hours
Neptune	2,788	165	30,775	8	16 hours
Pluto	3,667	248	1,485	1	6.4 days

The period of revolution refers to the time a planet takes to orbit the Sun.
The period of rotation is a planet's day.

THE NINE PLANETS

Beginning in the 1960s, unmanned space probes began to fly by, encircle, and even land on some of the planets, and our knowledge of our solar system became more concrete, certain, and comprehensive. In general, the planets fall into two categories. There are the terrestrial, or Earth-like, planets that formed close to the Sun and are composed of the heavier elements that form rocks and metals. These planets are Mercury, Venus, Earth, and Mars. The other planets, Jupiter, Saturn, Uranus, and Neptune, are called gas giants. They are huge balls of hydrogen and hydrogen compounds like methane and ammonia, and contain few heavy elements or metals. Pluto is a bit of an oddity, and may be nothing more than a small ball of frozen hydrogen. Some astronomers believe that Pluto should not be accorded the status of a planet at all. They believe it was a moon of Neptune that somehow escaped from its orbit. What else do we know about the planets?

Thirty-six million miles from the Sun lies Mercury, the innermost planet of our solar system. Mercury is difficult to observe because it is very near the Sun as seen from Earth. But in 1974, the spacecraft *Mariner 10* came within less than 1,000 kilometers of Mercury's surface and took 1,800 photographs. Mercury has no atmosphere, no rings, and no moons. Its surface is extremely hot, reaching more than 500° Celsius during the day. It is pockmarked by craters, like the Moon. It has only one-twentieth the mass of Earth, and at its surface, gravity is only one-third as strong as on Earth. It was once thought that Mercury, like Earth's moon, was locked into a pattern of "synchronous rotation." That is, it rotated once on its axis in the same time, eighty-eight days, than it took to revolve around the Sun. This would have meant that the same side of the planet always faces the Sun, just as the same side of the Moon always faces Earth. But Mercury does spin on its axis in less time, fifty-nine days, than it takes to orbit the Sun, and this was discovered through Doppler radar. The echo from a Doppler radar pulse not only tells you where an object is, but changes in the frequency of the returning pulse are used to measure whether that object is moving toward or away from the observer.

Only Pluto has a more eccentric orbit than Mercury. An orbit's eccentricity is a measure of how elliptical it is. All planets revolve in elliptical orbits, but most of these orbits are only slightly eccentric, that is, they are only slightly elliptical, and appear to be close to perfect circles. Mercury's orbit has a clearly discernable oval shape. This proved to be a boon to scientists trying to verify Albert Einstein's general theory of relativity after it was put forward in 1916. Einstein predicted that the perihelion of the orbit of planets would precess. That is, their elliptical orbits would slowly rotate. This was not an effect predicted by Newton's universal law of gravitation, and if this precession could be detected, it would prove that

Einstein's theory of gravity was a deeper and truer view of the universe than Newton's. But, as has been said, the orbits of most planets are too close to circular to measure this precession. A study of Mercury's orbit provided some of the evidence that led scientists to accept Einstein's radical ideas.

Venus is the second planet from the Sun and lies at a distance of 67 million miles from its star. It has about the same size and mass as Earth and is sometimes called our sister planet. Venus is surrounded by thick clouds, and though it is a very bright object in the sky, we can see little detail even with powerful optical telescopes. However, its surface has been mapped by ground-based radar, and both the United States and the former Soviet Union have sent more than a dozen spacecraft to explore the planet. Several probes have landed on its surface and survived the harsh conditions there for almost two hours. The atmosphere of Venus is primarily carbon dioxide and its clouds are composed of sulfuric acid.

The Pioneer Venus Orbiter *was lauched into an elliptical orbit around Venus in 1974. It carried a surface radar mapper to determine the planet's topography and surface characteristics.*

Its surface temperature is about 475° Celsius. Venus is considered an example of the runaway greenhouse effect that some environmentalists fear will one day drastically alter Earth's climate. The heavy concentration of carbon dioxide in the Venusian atmosphere traps the heat that the planet would normally radiate into space, raising surface temperatures to extreme levels. Venus has no moons or rings. In relation to the motions of the other planets, Venus rotates on its axis "the wrong way," and scientists still cannot explain this phenomenon.

Earth, as most of us know, is the third planet from the Sun, about 93 million miles away. There is no need to tell readers about Earth's atmosphere, its average temperatures, or the length of its day. Our planet is unique in that it is the only known planet on which water can exist in liquid form, and it is probably the only planet in the solar system on which there are living things. Scientists believe that these two facts are intimately connected. It also has a rather large moon. Earth is also a geologically active planet. Internal heat keeps layers of rock below the crust in a molten condition and produces thermal convection currents within the molten rock. This thermal convection is continually forcing up new sections of crust from below and destroying existing crust, and, in the process, creating forces that move continents.

THE SIZE OF THE SOLAR SYSTEM

From our perspective here, perhaps the most important fact about Earth is that it is the location from which we view the rest of the solar system and the universe. All our ideas about the cosmos, right or wrong, were based on observations made from this one place. So perhaps we should talk a bit about the "celestial sphere" that we see from Earth. The celestial sphere is the imaginary conception of the universe as the inner surface of a huge globe surrounding and rotating about Earth every twenty-four hours. The positions of all the stars and the planets can be marked if one can project some kind of grid system onto the inner surface of this sphere. What astronomers do is project onto the celestial sphere the same latitude and longitude lines as on Earth, but they give them different names. On the celestial sphere, latitude above or below the celestial equator, lying in the same plane as Earth's equator, is called declination, and longitude is known as right ascension. If you have had any experience working with an amateur telescope, then you are familiar with these terms.

Earth, of course, is rarely "upright" in relation to the solar plane, the plane extending outward from the Sun's equator, the plane in which the planets lie as they revolve around the Sun. Earth is tilted out of the vertical, in relation to the solar plane, by 23.5 degrees. As seen from Earth then, the Sun and the planets do not appear to revolve along the celestial equator, as the stars do, but along a diagonal line called the ecliptic. Along this ecliptic lie the twelve constellations of the zodiac, and the movement of the planets along this line through the various constellations, according to astrologers, determines our fate. As Earth moves around the Sun in its orbit, its tilt exposes different hemispheres to the direct rays of the Sun, so that Earth experiences seasonal changes in climate. In the present epoch, in the Northern Hemisphere, the axis of Earth is pointed toward a rather dim star called Polaris, the pole star. A time-exposed photograph would show that all the stars in the night sky appear to rotate around Polaris. If you can measure the number of degrees between Polaris and the southern horizon, and make an adjustment for your latitude, you can determine the degree of Earth's tilt from the ecliptic at any time of year.

Mars is the next planet from the Sun after Earth, at a distance of 142 million miles. A number of space-craft have landed on the surface of Mars and even chemically analyzed its soil. Iron oxide in the soil gives Mars its red color. Its atmosphere is a thin layer of carbon dioxide, and its surface is cold because of its distance from the Sun. There is evidence that Mars had liquid water on its surface millions of years ago, and some of that water may still be trapped in the polar ice caps or beneath the surface of the planet. For this reason, scientists are deeply interested in Mars as the possible abode of life. But so far all the evidence is either negative or inconclusive. Mars has two relatively small moons, Phobus and Deimos. Mars has a rigid crust not affected by underlying currents of liquid rock, and it is generally considered a geologically

The undeployed Sojourner Rover sits on Mars in thi[s] image taken on the day it landed

inactive planet. Yet there is evidence of great volcanic activity in the past. Mars's axis of rotation is tilted off "vertical" to just about the same degree as Earth's axis, so that Mars experiences seasonal variations in weather just like Earth. But because of its greater distance from the Sun and its larger orbit, the Martian year is 686 days long.

THE SIZE OF THE SOLAR SYSTEM

Beyond Mars is Jupiter, 484 million miles from the Sun. Jupiter and the other outer planets are very different in nature from the inner planets. When the primordial cloud of gas and dust was collapsing to form the solar system, the heavier elements—carbon, silicon, iron, and nickel—the "dust," were pulled inward to form the inner planets, which are hard and rocky and metallic. Jupiter was formed from the remaining light elements, mostly hydrogen and helium. In terms of its chemistry, Jupiter resembles the Sun more than it resembles an inner planet. And some astronomers believe that Jupiter is an example of a "failed star," a ball of gas that was not quite large enough to condense to the point where gravitational pressure could ignite a fusion reaction. And like a star, Jupiter has its own mini-solar system, with seventeen moons. Some of the larger moons, including Io and Europa, are extremely interesting to scientists. Io shows evidence of current volcanic activity. Europa is currently thought to have an ocean of liquid water trapped beneath a crust of ice, and this is considered a likely place to look for life. Jupiter also has a thin ring like Saturn. Jupiter is more than 300 times as massive as Earth. Though its surface layers are gaseous, most of the interior of Jupiter consists of highly compressed liquid hydrogen. In this state, hydrogen can conduct electricity, and we know that Jupiter has a very strong magnetic field. The core of Jupiter is also generating heat; in fact, it is thought to be generating twice as much heat as the planet receives from the Sun. This heat drives a spectacular weather system featuring colorful bands of clouds and massive storms (such as the great red spot) that last for centuries.

Saturn, Uranus, and Neptune are also gas giants and similar in composition to Jupiter. Saturn is almost 900 million miles from the Sun and takes thirty Earth years to revolve around the Sun. Because of its rings, it is considered by many astronomers to be the most beautiful object in the solar system. Saturn also has twenty-two moons. Uranus and Neptune are both fairly large planets, about 30,000 miles in diameter compared to a diameter of 8,000 miles for Earth. Uranus takes 84 Earth years to revolve around the Sun, and Neptune takes more than 164 years to complete its orbit. Both Uranus and Neptune have rings. Uranus is unusual in that its axis of rotation is almost 90 degrees off "vertical." It is literally rotating on its side as it circles the Sun. Uranus has twenty-one moons, and Neptune has eight.

Pluto is the smallest and most distant planet in the solar system, more than 3.6 billion miles from the Sun. Pluto takes 248 Earth years to circle the Sun. Unlike the gas giants, it is probably mostly solid ice of some kind. It has one moon, Charon. Because Charon is about the same size and mass as Pluto, it is sometimes called a "companion" rather than a moon, and Pluto itself has had a hard time earning the title of a planet. Its orbit is very eccentric, sometimes bringing Pluto within the orbit of Neptune. Some astronomers think it is an escaped moon of Neptune.

OTHER OBJECTS IN OUR SOLAR SYSTEM

Other objects in our solar system include comets, asteroids, and meteoroids. Comets are believed to be composed of the rocks, dust, and icy matter left over from the formation of the solar system. In 1949, American astronomer Fred Whipple (1906–) suggested that they were conglomerates of dust mixed with frozen water, carbon dioxide, ammonia, and methane. Whipple's theory of comets is sometimes called the "dirty snowball" theory. Though some comets sweep very close to the Sun in their orbits, their home territory is the Oort cloud, a ring of debris about nine billion miles from the Sun, six billion miles beyond the orbit of Pluto. Dutch astronomer Jan Hendrik Oort (1900–1992) proposed the existence of this belt of primordial material in 1950. From time to time a gravitational perturbation in the solar system will pull a chunk of this debris from its distant ring into a close orbit around the Sun. Heat and radiation pressure from the

This image of Halley's comet was photographed from New South Wales, Australia in 1985.

Sun vaporize some of the comet's icy material and push it out into a spectacular tail that always faces away from the Sun, no matter in what direction in its orbit the comet is traveling. Comets can orbit near enough to Earth to be seen over and over again. An example is Halley's comet, which last came within Earth's view in 1986 and has a period of seventy-six years.

Searching for new comets is a painstaking process of looking for new and very faint objects in the night sky. For this reason, it is not an activity that attracts the efforts of many professional astronomers. Many new comets are discovered by amateur astronomers working with less-powerful telescopes, and comet hunting is a good way to develop a young person's interest in astronomy and teach that person how to use a telescope.

Asteroids are rocky objects, smaller than planets, that orbit the Sun. Tens of thousands of them are found between Mars and Jupiter in the so-called asteroid belt. Originally it was believed that all these asteroids located between Mars and Jupiter were the remains of a planet that had broken up or never formed for some reason. That theory is no longer considered valid because different groups of these asteroids have very different chemical compositions. Some asteroids are rocky in nature. Others have greater concentrations of carbon, and still others are composed mostly of iron

The hardy Pioneer 10 *spacecraft passed by Jupiter in 1973 and was still communicating with Earth as recently as April 2001.*

and nickel. It is unlikely that they originated in the same body. Asteroids can vary in size from as small as one kilometer in diameter to objects as large as the planets' moons. The largest asteroid discovered so far is Ceres, almost 700 miles in diameter.

Spacecraft have allowed us to get closer looks at asteroids. *Pioneer 10* was the first spacecraft to travel through the asteroid belt. In 2000, another spacecraft, the *NEAR-Shoemaker*, flew within four miles of the asteroid called Eros. Eros is about twenty-two miles long and about 100 million miles from Earth. Instruments onboard the *NEAR* will allow scientists to learn more about the composition of asteroids.

Small chunks of rocky material, or large clouds of such material, ranging from pebble-size objects to those tens of meters in diameter, can be found all over the solar system. In space they are known as meteoroids. When Earth travels through a cloud of such objects and they enter the atmosphere,

The inset image above is an artist's conception of the asteroid impact that may have caused the extinction of many species during the Cretaceous era. The Moon's surface, at right, is covered with such impact craters.

producing bright trails of light as they burn up, they are called meteors. If a meteoroid is big enough so that it doesn't all burn up in the atmosphere, the remaining fragment that reaches Earth is called a meteorite. Meteors may be rocky or metallic and can weigh as much as several thousand pounds. Meteor showers occur at different times of the year, but there are some meteor showers that occur regularly, like the Perseids, which reach a maximum around August 12. The surfaces of planets and moons without atmospheres to burn up such objects are covered with the impact craters of meteorites.

Other Solar Systems

As new and more powerful telescopes have become available, including space-based observation platforms like the Hubble Space Telescope, astronomers have had the means to explore one of the most intriguing questions that arose from the study of our solar system.

The two domes of the twin ten-meter Keck telescopes tower atop Mauna Kea on the island of Hawaii.

Are there other solar systems or other systems of planets orbiting other stars? Do they resemble our solar system, and is it possible that life exists on other planets and has built a technological civilization such as ours?

Astronauts repair the Hubble Space Telescope.

How would one go about detecting a planet orbiting another star? Even the closest stars are so far away that they are mere points of light, seen only because they are so bright. Except for the Sun, the actual physical dimensions of stars are not observed by us, even with telescopes. But in recent years astronomers have devised some very sophisticated methods for suggesting the existence of new planets.

One method involves a careful analysis of a star's motion, using parallax measurements, spectroscopy, and astrophotography, to determine if it is gravitationally bound to another object.

Stars have several kinds of motion that must be ignored before these measurements can be made. The "apparent motion" of a star is its movement from east to west across the sky as a result of Earth's rotation. Telescopes can be fitted with clock mechanisms that enable them to track stars across the sky, so that this motion does not trouble the observer. But the observer must also know if the star has a "proper motion," that is, a movement relative to our solar system, to the right or left, up or down, or toward or away from us. Motions across our field of vision can be measured by careful comparison of photographic plates taken over time. Motions toward or away from us can be measured by Doppler shifts in the frequency of the light coming from a star. After these motions are accounted for, astronomers look for another

In the beginning there was nothing but hydrogen and helium gas. Then gravity caused clumps of this gas to contract and form stars and planets. But we are composed of heavier elements than hydrogen and helium. We are composed of elements like carbon, oxygen, and nitrogen, and our planet is composed of heavier elements like silicon, iron, nickel, and uranium. Where did these elements come from?

Stars are born and stars die. When they have used up all their fuel, some stars experience massive explosions that fuse lighter elements into heavier elements, and these heavier elements are then blown all across the universe to become part of other gas clouds that are contracting to form new stars. Our sun, only 5 billion years old in a universe that is about 15 billion years old, is a late generation star, formed from a cloud of gas that was already contaminated with the heavier elements from other, ancient stellar explosions. But were it not for the death of those older stars, there would be no rocky planets in our solar system and no life as we know it. The Sun is known as a Population I star and contains a certain amount of heavy elements. Older stars are called Population II stars, and they have a chemical composition quite different from our sun. Around such older stars, one would not expect to find Earth-like planets.

Top: the Ring Nebula, remnant of a supernova
Left: a flare on the surface of the Sun

motion, a tiny wobble or oscillation in the star's position, detected either through parallax or Doppler shifts, that seems to indicate that a star is revolving in tandem with another object.

In October 1995, Michel Mayor and Didier Queloz of the Geneva Observatory in Switzerland detected the first planet believed to be orbiting another star. The star was 51 Pegasi in the constellation Pegasus, a star not too different from our own sun, about forty-two light-years from Earth. The astronomers detected a Doppler shift in the star's light that indicated that another object was revolving around it every 4.2 days. That object was half the size of Jupiter and revolved around its star four times faster than Earth revolves around the Sun. Astronomers then studied 300 stars similar to the Sun, all within fifty light-years of Earth, and turned up evidence of eight new planets. Overall, we now suspect that there are solar systems around fifty stars containing at least sixty-three planets. Most are very large planets, like the gas giants in our solar system, and many orbit very close to their stars, closer than Mercury is to our sun. So these solar systems appear "abnormal" compared to our solar system, where the large planets are farther away from their star. All this raises many new questions about how solar systems evolve.

Astronomers have also found evidence that many stars are surrounded by an "accretion disk" of gas and dust, which indicates that planets may be in the process of formation around them. The star Beta Pictoris was found to have such a ring of material around it as early as 1983. More recent observations by the Hubble Space Telescope seem to indicate that a planet has already formed and is causing gravitational distortions in the accretion disk. Observing with radio telescopes, astronomers have studied a gas cloud known as Bok Globule B335 and discovered gas and dust collapsing onto a new star that is only about 150,000 years old. Bok globules, named for Bart Bok, the astronomer who studied them, are unusually dark clouds that seem to be the sites of star formation.

The dark spots in this photograph are Bok globules, which are clouds of dust and gas where new stars are formed

What is particularly exciting about these discoveries is that they confirm the nebular hypothesis put forward by Kant and Laplace to explain how solar systems originate in a cloud of collapsing gas. What is particularly frustrating about all these discoveries is that none of the planets so far detected around other stars resemble Earth or any other terrestrial-type planet. Is an Earth-type planet a rarity when new solar systems form? If so, the chances for discovering life elsewhere in the universe are not so good. The evidence so far seems to indicate that solar systems form quite commonly, as one would expect if our theory of their formation is correct. Does the evidence also suggest that only large, lifeless gas giants like Jupiter form around stars? That is hard to say. We detect these types of planets precisely because they are so massive and because they have a detectable gravitational effect on their star. Small, Earth-like planets would be very difficult to detect even if they were present. The answer may have to wait until we have more powerful telescopes or more sophisticated methods of testing our ideas.

Glossary

asteroid A small, rocky object that orbits the Sun between Mars and Jupiter.

astronomical unit The mean distance from Earth to the Sun, 93 million miles.

celestial equator The intersection of the celestial sphere with the plane that passes through Earth's equator.

circumference The perimeter of a circle.

comet An object composed of rock, dust, and ice that orbits the Sun with a long tail of incandescent gas visible from Earth.

eccentricity   A mathematical measure of the shape of an ellipse that quantifies its difference from a perfect circle.

eclipse   The total or partial obscuring of one celestial body by another.

ecliptic   The path followed by the Sun across the celestial sphere in the course of a year.

ellipse   An oval-shaped curve formed as a cross-sectional plane cut through a cone.

equinox   An intersection between the ecliptic and the celestial equator. When the Sun is on this point, day and night are equal in length.

heliocentric   Sun-centered.

meteor   A small chunk of rocky or metallic material that reaches Earth's atmosphere and burns up (often called a shooting star).

nuclear fusion   A process whereby light atomic nuclei combine to form a heavier nucleus, releasing energy in the process.

parallax The angular shift in position of a celestial body when measured from two separate points.

radioactive Exhibiting nuclear decay by the spontaneous emission of radiation.

retrograde Having motion opposite to that of other celestial bodies.

revolution The orbiting of one object around another.

rotation The spinning of a body around its own axis.

solstice The point on the celestial sphere indicating the northernmost or southernmost declination or height of the Sun during a year, marking the longest and shortest days of the year.

zenith The point vertically above an observer on the surface of Earth.

for More Information

ORGANIZATIONS

International Astronomical Union
Central Bureau for Astronomical Telegrams
Smithsonian Astrophysical Observatory
Cambridge, MA 02138
(617) 864-5758
Web site: http://www.iau.org
This is the organization to contact if you think you have
discovered a new comet.

MAGAZINES

Astronomy
21027 Crossroads Circle
P.O. Box 1612
Waukesha, WI 53187-1612
Web site: http://www.astronomy.com/home.asp

Sky and Telescope
49 Bay State Road
Cambridge, MA 02138
(800) 253-0245
Web site: http://www.skypub.com

WEB SITES

Astronomical Society of the Pacific
http://www.aspsky.org

Imagine the Universe! (a NASA educational site)
http://imagine.gsfc.nasa.gov

FOR MORE INFORMATION

NASA Spacelink
http://spacelink.nasa.gov

Nine Planets
http://www.nineplanets.org

The Planetary Society
http://planetary.org

Solar System Simulator
http://space.jpl.nasa.gov

Virtual Solar System
http://www.nationalgeographic.com/solarsystem

For Further Reading

Filkin, David. *Stephen Hawking's Universe: The Cosmos Explained.* New York: Basic Books, 1998.

Friedman, Herbert. *The Astronomer's Universe: Stars, Galaxies, and Cosmos.* New York: W. W. Norton & Company, 1998.

Goldsmith, Donald. *Worlds Unnumbered: The Search for Extrasolar Planets.* Sausalito, CA: University Science Books, 1997.

Levy, David H., ed. *The Scientific American Book of the Cosmos.* New York: St. Martin's Press, 2000.

Maran, Stephen P. *Astronomy for Dummies.* Foster City, CA: IDG Books Worldwide, Inc., 1999.

FOR FURTHER READING

Raymo, Chet. *365 Starry Nights: An Introduction to Astronomy for Every Night of the Year.* New York: Simon & Schuster, 1992.

Stern, S. Alan. *Our Worlds: The Magnetism and Thrill of Planetary Exploration.* New York: Cambridge University Press, 1999.

Wunsch, Susi Trautmann. *The Adventures of Sojourner: The Mission to Mars That Thrilled the World.* New York: Mikaya Press, 1998.

Index

Credits

ABOUT THE AUTHOR

Isaac Turiel received his doctorate in physics from New York University. He conducted research in X-ray astronomy before taking a teaching position at the University of California at Berkeley, where he also worked on energy efficiency at the university's Lawrence National Laboratory. He has written two books and numerous articles on technical subjects.

PHOTO CREDITS

Cover © John Foster/Photo Researchers; cover inset © ©Roger Ressmeyer/Corbis.; pp. 8, 13, 32, 35, 37, 49, 51 © Northwind Picture Archives; p. 9 © Peter Adams/FPG;

p. 11 © Bill Livingston/AURA/NOAO/NSF; p. 14 © Corbis; pp. 48, 79, 80, 81 © PhotoDisc; pp. 38, 39, 40, 58, 61 © Bettmann/Corbis; pp. 44, 53 © Archive Photos; p. 60 © Dave G. Houser/Corbis; p. 67 © NSSDC/NASA; p. 72 © Pathfinder, JPL/NASA; p. 77 © Popperfoto/Archive Photo; pp. 84–85 © W. M. Keck Observatory; p. 86 © NASA; p. 88–89 © SOHO-EIT Consortuim, ESA, NASA; p. 89 © Subaru 8.3m Telescope, NAOJ; p. 92 © Anglo-Australian Telescope photograph by David Malin. Diagrams on pp. 16, 18, 21, 26, 41 by Geri Giordano.

DESIGN AND LAYOUT

Evelyn Horovicz